Oxford Past and Present

FORTIS EST VERITAS

Oxford Past and Present

COMPILED BY

C.W.Judge

THE OXFORD
ILLUSTRATED PRESS

Printed in the City of Oxford by B. H. Blackwell Ltd, 1970
Reprinted 1971
Type set by Holywell Press Ltd., Oxford
Bound by Henry Brooks Ltd., Bookbinders, Oxford

Acknowledgements:—
The Bodleian Library for permission to use the photographs from
the Harry Minn collection. Adrian Lack for taking the new
pictures of Oxford. Miss M. Nichols for revising this edition.
Local firms for their co-operation in the preparation of this book.
City of Oxford Libraries for the loan of the old map and photo-
graphs (Pages 1, 23, 46, 54) from the Taunt collection. City of
Oxford Motor Services for their help.

SBN 902280 00 7

Preface

THIS book was conceived when I was lucky enough to see part of the Harry Minn collection of photographs, now in the Bodleian Library. Looking through the multitude of books about Oxford I found a complete lack of pictorial reference to the City, its streets, buildings and alleyways. I hope that this book will help fill the gap.

The main picture on each page is from the Minn collection, taken about the turn of the century, during a more leisured age. The smaller new photographs have been taken—wherever possible—from the exact spot where Harry Minn's camera may have stood.

Whilst preparing this book I stumbled across several interesting facts associated with the pictures, and we have endeavoured to include as many of these as space will permit in the captions. The Minn Collection is vast in extent, almost all of Oxford having been photographed; it is impossible therefore, for me to include reproductions of every plate. I hope that my selection is an interesting one and will help to show how much our city has changed during this century.

At the end of the book I have included several early advertisements of well established Oxford companies and on page 56 is a map to help identify the position of the photographs.

Finally, I would like to thank Nicholas Owen for writing the text and helping with the research and everybody who has been connected with this interesting project.

Oxford 1970   COLIN JUDGE

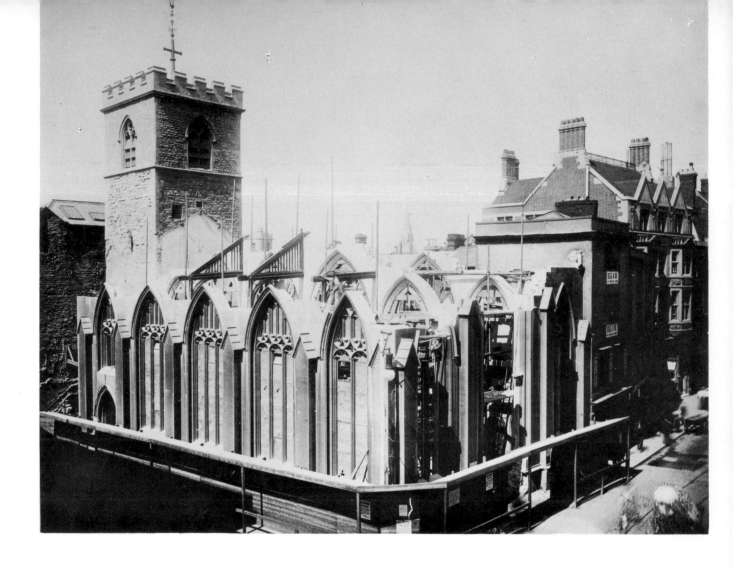

Now spacious enough to be a roomy and popular meeting place, Carfax was once a narrow crossroads, most light being excluded by tall, ancient buildings. At the end of the last century a large church stood on the NW corner, now a wide, flagged pavement.

Demolished in 1896 because of the Carfax Improvement Scheme, St. Martin's origins are lost in history. Its name first appeared in contemporary records of 1032. All the medieval building, except the tower which still stands, was demolished in 1819 to make way for a new building which was erected during 1820-1822. St. Martin's Church windows were used in the reconstruction of St. Clement's Church and part of St. Martin's old churchyard now forms a tranquil garden in central Oxford.

Although an elegant pre-Second World War building now replaces the old nondescript one at the corner of the Broad and Cornmarket, most of the businesses have survived.

The Oxford Drug Company still occupies the same site as it did in the 1890's, although they have extended their premises around the back of Baker's new store. Buckell and Ballard now have their offices by Carfax after being first in King Edward Street and then in Cornmarket. Note how the ancient tower of St. Michael's is now dwarfed by the new corner building.

In 1885 Gloucester Green was still used as a cattle market, the north side of it taken up by a row of decrepit houses. Not long after the above photograph was taken, these cottages were pulled down to make way for the old Central Boys' School. When the cattle market was moved to the present site at the Oxpens, the school became the offices and waiting room for the City of Oxford Motor Services, who lease half the 'Green' as a Country Bus Station. Near this area is the coach station from which coaches take travellers to all parts of Great Britain

3

Little remains to identify this view of Worcester Street and Hythe Bridge Street. Even the Oxford Castle tower seems to have shrunk behind Nuffield College. In the above photograph all seems quiet, yet around the corner, past the garage, was a hump-back bridge—demolished quite recently—which crossed the old Oxford Canal at its terminal wharf. The entrance to George Street, now much widened, is at present bordered on the north side by a Municipal Restaurant—still an ugly wartime 'temporary building'—and to the south by a modern block of shops and offices.

9th July 1914, in Queen Street, the Electra Cinema was still a novelty and the Air Balloon had a large number of regular patrons. Now the latter and the neighbouring buildings have been replaced by Council Offices, and the former, whose doors closed about a decade ago, has become a large Co-operative store. Happily, however, a great many of the buildings' façades remain unspoilt.

The Grapes public house still looks across George Street onto a theatre. Indeed, it is still 'The New' which it sees but there the resemblance ends. Now, instead of an old, shabby theatre with Edwardian awning and gas lamps, a new theatre—one of the finest in the provinces—stands testament that Oxford still enjoys a stage production. The New Theatre was built in the 1930's and is noted for an unbroken run of Christmas pantomimes at which a million children, some now parents themselves, have laughed.

At one time the approach to the GWR and LMS stations was the western terminus for the Oxford Tramways Company and the old track can be plainly seen in this photograph of Park End Street. Both the Railway Hotel and the Robin Hood have disappeared to make room for the new Royal Oxford Hotel, opened in November 1935. Gone too, are the old subterranean toilets, moved to the other side of the station in a road improvement scheme at the end of the 1950's. Until recently the railings of the old station yard were covered with enamelled metal advertisements for *Gold Leaf Cigarettes, Ronuk Polish, Wright's Coal Tar Soap* and many other products, some still being manufactured, some forgotten—as is the old station, now a coal dump, goods yard and motor car tyre depot.

This view of Worcester Street remained almost unchanged until after the Second World War when increased traffic made it impossible for the little street to handle all the extra vehicles. In the left foreground, the Queen's Arms is the only remaining building. Once this area was a hive of commercial activity, with wharfs at the terminus of the old Oxford Canal to left and right behind the high walls. Now all is gone and replaced by a new college and huge car park.

St. George's Church was consecrated on 30th November, 1849 and demolished in 1935 to make way for the ABC Cinema (then called The Ritz). The church site was bought for £1,250 and it was built at a cost of about £4,500. Before being demolished it served as Oxford's Labour Exchange. The ABC, the city's largest and best equipped cinema, had one of the finest cinema organs in England.

Long forgotten are the toll gates at The Plain reminding one that the High Road from Wales and Cheltenham to London once passed directly through Oxford. Magdalen Bridge, still a vital link between Central and East Oxford, has remained as it was and somehow even today reflects the calm of the River Cherwell which flows beneath it.

Dec. 1913

Oxford Motor Omnibus Co.

MOTOR BUSES

WILL RUN BETWEN

The Stations and Cowley Terminus

ON AND AFTER

FRIDAY, DECEMBER 5

WEEK DAYS.

The first Buses will leave Cowley Terminus and the Stations at 7.40 a.m., and continue to run every 20 minutes until 11 p.m.

SUNDAYS.

The first Buses will leave Cowley Terminus and the Stations at 2 p.m. and the last Buses at 10.20 p.m.

Further Particulars will be announced shortly.

W. R. MORRIS, Manager.

HOLYWELL PRESS, LTD., OXFORD.

OXFORD LOCAL BOARD.

NOTICE

To Persons removing Night Soil.

No Night Soil, Sewage, or contents of a Cesspool, nor any other noxious matter shall be got out of or removed from any Cesspool, Privy, or place of Deposit, nor conveyed through any Street, except between the hours of 12 o'clock at night and 5 o'clock in the morning, from the 30th of September to the 31st of March, and between the hours of 12 o'clock at night and 4 o'clock in the morning, during the remainder of the year.

No Night Soil or other matter aforesaid, shall be conveyed through the Streets except in Carts or Vessels properly covered and secured against any escape of the contents thereof, or any issue of offensive smells from the same.

If in emptying any Privy, Watercloset or Cesspool, or removing Night Soil, any such Night Soil, contents, or other offensive matter shall be dropped, spilled, or slopped in any Street, the Persons engaged in such emptying or removal shall carefully sweep and cleanse the place on which the same shall have been dropped, and remove the sweepings therefrom, between the hours hereinbefore named.

No cart, waggon, carriage or vessel, used for the purpose of receiving and removing Night Soil, Sewage, or other such matter as aforesaid, shall be suffered to remain in any Street for any longer time than shall be necessary for the loading and unloading thereof.

All Persons offending against any of the foregoing Regulations are liable to a Penalty not exceeding £5, and in case of a continuing offence, to a further Penalty not exceeding 40s. a day, after written notice of the offence from the Local Board or their authorised Officer.

FREDERICK J. MORRELL,

Clerk to the Board.

1a, S. Giles', Oxford,
July 5th, 1871.

UPSTONE & DOE, PRINTERS, 16½, QUEEN STREET, OXFORD.

CLARENDON HOTEL STABLES, OXFORD.

SALE OF

ALDERNEY, GUERNSEY, & JERSEY

HEIFERS.

MESSRS. T. MALLAM & SON

Have received instructions from Mr. EDWARD PARSONS FOWLER, the eminent Exporter and Purveyor to the Royal Dairies at Windsor and Osborne, to

SELL BY AUCTION,

IN THE YARD OF THE CLARENDON HOTEL, OXFORD,

ON

SATURDAY, March 21, 1868, at 2 for 3 o'clock,

A VERY SUPERIOR HERD OF ELEVEN IN-CALF AND DOWN-CALVING

COWS AND HEIFERS,

Of great beauty, selected and Exported expressly for this Sale from the choicest herds in the Islands.

ALDERNEYS & JERSEYS.

Lot	Age	Expected Calving date.	Colour.	Remarks.
1.	2 yrs.	April	Grey and White........	Very handsome.
2.	3 yrs.	March	Brown and little white	A colour choice.
3.	2 yrs.	March	Pure Fawn	Prize heifer
4.	2 yrs.	April	Grey and white.........	A match pair and the choicest ever exported.
5.	2 yrs.	March	Grey and white	
6.	4 yrs.	April	Fawn, grey, & white ...	A magnificent cow.
7.	3 yrs.	March	Red and grey...........	A beautiful show.

GUERNSEYS.

8.	2 yrs.		Yellow and white......	A pair of heifers for breeding invaluable.
9.	2 yrs.		Yellow and white......	
10.	3 yrs.		Brindle and white	A grand show.
11.	3 yrs.		Yellow and white......	A splendid cow.

Selected and imported with extreme care from the choicest herds on the Islands, expressly for this Sale by the sole and only resident exporter,

MR. EDWARD PARSONS FOWLER,

of Jersey, (Purveyor to the Royal Dairies,) exporting annually 1000 from the Islands for the last 30 years, and whose celebrity as a judge will be a sufficient guarantee of the superiority of the animals, rejecting inferior Cattle, and personally selecting his importations.

Preference is now universally given to the above Breed of Cattle for Dairy purposes, their superior and prolific milking qualities recommending them wherever they have been exported to.

On View the Morning of Sale.

The Auctioneer will commence precisely at Three o'clock

Printed at the Offices of the Oxford Chronicle Company (Limited.)

CITY OF OXFORD.

GLOUCESTER GREEN FAIR.

NOTICE IS HEREBY GIVEN,

That no Caravan, or other Carriage, will be permitted to enter the Fair until such Caravan or Carriage has been inspected by Mr Thomas Hull, the Sanitary Inspector of the Corporation, and until permission in writing has been granted by the said Inspector.

That no Caravan or other Carriage, nor any Materials for erecting Stands or Stalls in or around the Cattle Market, shall be left to stand in any of the Streets, Lanes, or Public Highways, before the hour of Six o'clock on Friday Morning, May 3rd, or after the hour of Seven o'clock on the Morning of Saturday, May 4th.

No Booth, Stand, or Stall will be permitted, unless previous permission be obtained from Mr. John Beckwith, Mayor's Sergeant, Town Hall, Oxford, to whom payment for such Standing must previously be made according to the Authorized Scale of Charges.

EDMUND JOHN BROOKS,

MAYOR.

Oxford, April 18th, 1907.

Printed by James Parker and Co., Crown Yard, Oxford.

Looking south down St. Aldate's, many narrow streets, yards and alleys have disappeared. The three buildings in the right foreground are still there, exactly as they were; indeed, one is still a Co-operative Store. Now all the houses to the left of this road have been demolished to form a car park and a wide new inner relief road has been built, linking St. Aldate's with the Oxpens and the railway station.

One of the first streets of houses to be pulled down in the old St. Ebbe's area was Speedwell Street, off St. Aldate's, just north of Folly Bridge. On the approach from St. Aldate's there is only one house, common to both photographs, that remains standing. The new building to the left of the modern photograph is Oxford's new telephone exchange.

At one time, the early Georgian façade of the Old Town Hall housed the Oxford Wine Company, the Post Office (opened in 1842), and the first Free Library in Oxford whose first librarian was Mr. B. H. Blackwell. Now, a Victorian front replaces the simple lines of a gentler age. The wine company is defunct, the Post Office has moved to the other side of St. Aldate's, and Blackwell's are selling books worldwide, rather than lending them just to Oxford.

15

Catte Street as it appeared from the south around 1880. Now all the small shops have disappeared; indeed the top photograph shows them being destroyed. This corner is now taken up by a building erected in 1903 belonging to Hertford College and joined to the main part of it by the famous bridge. What used to be The Indian Institute, on the corner of Holywell, is now occupied by administrative offices of the University.

Castle Street in August 1913. Most of these buildings were demolished in 1968 to make room for the Westgate Shopping Centre, an area of development consisting of shops, a car park and the new public library. On the right of the street in 1913 was The Oxford Electric Theatre where, a year before, one could have seen a film entitled 'The Great Indian Massacre' which a contemporary advertisement in the Oxford Times said, 'Portrayed scenes of atrocities carried on in India'. The cinema became a Council canteen before being demolished.

St. Ebbe's in August 1913 was virtually the same as it was at the end of the last war. David Duce still sold fish there and Butler's Meat Store had become a pet food store where you could buy sunflower seeds for parrots, cuttlefish shells, dried ant's eggs and fresh horse-meat. Now Cooper's shop front dominates the west side of the street, although halfway down it remains the same. The east side, however, has completely changed—with shops under the Council offices that have their entrances in St. Ebbe's Street. The St. Ebbe's Cash Drapery Store is now a furniture store.

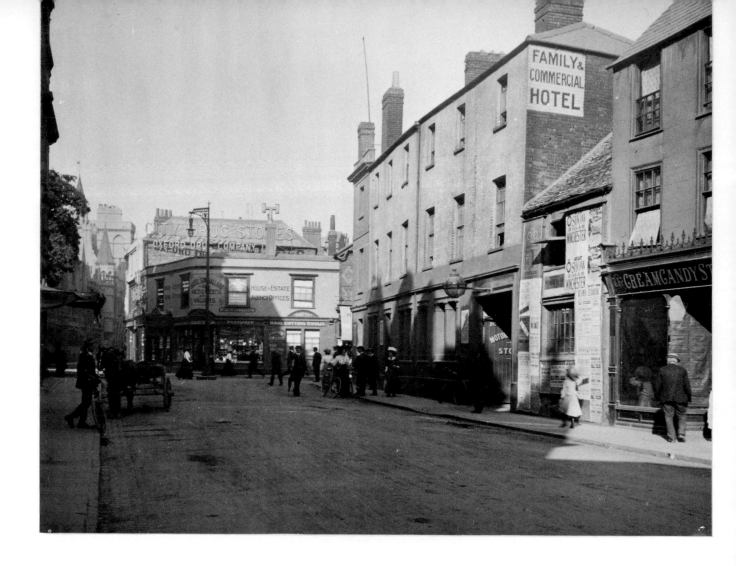

Now a modern branch of the National Westminster Bank, this corner used to be The George Street Family Hotel, formerly called The Three Goats. Here again can be seen the difference that William Baker, the furnishers, has made to this corner.

Another view of St. Aldate's, this time from the south. In the early 19th century, it was a very narrow street but now, with the Police Station and gardens on one side and The Morris Garages on the other, a change, perhaps for the better, can be noticed if only because it affords visitors a far better view of Tom Tower.

New College can be plainly seen in this 1913 photograph of New College Lane, shortly before the construction of the bridge, which is shown in the bottom picture. The bridge links the two parts of Hertford College.

21

The north-east corner of Carfax showing the north side of High Street.

The ornate façade of the Lloyd's Bank building has changed this aspect beyond recognition. Slatter and Rose moved further down The High and Goold and Sons now have their office in Worcester Street.

Broad, wide and level streets were one of the criteria for consideration when a group of London businessmen decided to form a tram company in Oxford during the late nineteenth century. On the 1st December 1881 the first part of a 5¼ mile network was opened by the Mayor, Sheriff and a number of citizens who journeyed from the station to Magdalen Road in Cowley.

Oxford was a busy place even in those days, with an estimated population of 40,000, the majority living in the suburbs, with the centre of the city mostly taken up with University property. It had a term-time population of more than 2,500 undergraduates. Also to be transported to and from the surrounding districts was the daily average of 2,500 people using the Great Western and London and North Western Railways. Basically, there were two main tramways planned. The first to operate was the east-west line, from the station to the Cowley Road where the Regal Cinema now stands. This, as well as linking the station with the centre of Oxford, also served the most densely populated area of the city.

The second line, completed in its entirety and opened to the public on 5th December, 1898, linked the city from the north to south—from South Parade on the Banbury Road to Lake Street in New Hinksey. This line ensured regular transport to those who lived in the new, growing areas it passed through.

Engineered by John Brunton, the system took the form of a 4' gauge, single line track, with passing loops, and double track along The High. Its main depot was at Leopold Street off the Cowley Road and there were also secondary depots at Jericho House, Walton Street, The Cape of Good Hope on The Plain, and at the Brewer Street Stables, St. Aldate's. There was rolling stock of 16 single deck cars, with seats lengthwise along the sides, which carried 20 to 25 passengers. The Company also owned 99 horses.

By 1900, 56,000 people were being carried annually. There were no 'stops', the public being able 'to hail a passing cab' wherever they chose along its route. As there was a speed limit of 8 mph one supposes that most people just hopped on. By 1910 the Company was running 19 trams and owned 150 horses. They also ran various horse buses to serve the outlying villages of Iffley, Cowley and Headington. An independent company was running a service from the bottom of Cumnor Hill via Osney to George Street.

In 1905 it was proposed to electrify the tramway. The University, ever wary of ruining the beauty and serenity of its precincts, immediately discouraged any form of power systems which employed an overhead electrical supply. A public meeting was held in the Town Hall in January 1906, where the Council's aim that the tramway should be electrified was defeated (one assumes by a purely University majority). However, the Council took over the horse-powered system on 6th December of that year and immediately introduced plans to lay new track, mainly along St. Clements, Headington Road, Iffley Road and an extension along the Banbury Road to Hernes Road North. This would have nearly doubled the tramways but it never happened because, without electrical power, the trams were dying a natural death—superseded by the faster, more versatile, motor bus. Before the first World War, even Lord Nuffield (then W. R. Morris), had a small bus company. He was the man who really made Oxford and the district of Cowley the prosperous place it is today, by starting the motor car factory at Cowley after commencing business in a small way as a builder of bicycles. His company operated services from Cowley Road to the station, Broad Street to Iffley, Cornmarket to Hayfield Road, via Walton Street, and Carfax to Wolvercote and New Hinksey. He introduced fixed stops with the familiar red and blue signs. At first, as he could not get licences for his buses, Morris could not sell tickets from the vehicles, so payment was made to agents where coupons were issued. Records show that after only four days 17,000 people had been carried—the trams being virtually deserted. Motor buses gained strength from strength. Slowly, the City of Oxford Motor Service took over opposition until today it operates a comprehensive service in Oxford and surrounding districts.

Another view of The George Hotel and the west side of Cornmarket. This shows that the buildings have hardly changed at all, except for the Clarendon Hotel which has now been replaced by Woolworth's new building. It is interesting to note that what is now the corner Elliston and Cavell Men's Shop was at one time a Freeman Hardy and Willis shoe store. The tramlines may be clearly seen.

The west side of Magdalen Street showing C. Taphouse and Son still in their present location. The shop next door was the original premises of Emberlin the stationers, now situated in Turl Street. Above their premises was the Registry of Male and Female Servants whose telephone number was Oxford 1. This building has now been pulled down and replaced with the department store of Elliston and Cavell Limited.

St. Aldate's taken from Speedwell Street looking south. This photograph was taken in 1910 and shows the same aspect as the photograph on page 20 but from the other direction. Clearly marked is Floyds Row, now the corner of the Thames Valley Divisional Police Headquarters, along which the Ministry of Labour building is situated.

Cornmarket showing the old Clarendon Hotel which was closed to the public after the Press Ball of 1939. Formerly called the Star Hotel, it provided lodgings for judges and lawyers in Oxford for the Assizes until their new lodgings were built in St. Giles. Before the last war this hotel was famous as a popular meeting place for both townspeople and members of the University. After its wartime function as a servicemen's mess, the Clarendon was finally demolished to make way for F. W. Woolworth's new building.

In 1908 the south side of The High below Oriel Street did not contain the grandeur of the Rhodes building of Oriel College but had a row of pleasing Georgian houses converted into shops. Queen's College can be clearly seen in both photographs, as can the sycamore tree which has not yet fallen in the name of progress. A good view of the tramline may be seen and it is said that grass grew between its rails during the long vacation.

29

Frank Cooper's factory, home of the famous *Oxford Marmalade*, has now moved from the old, gaunt buildings it used to occupy in Park End Street. Their place has been taken by the County Council. Gone, too, from the other corner, is Hall's Oxford Brewery. Both these firms—originally Oxonian—have been taken over and no longer exist in their original names.

Another view of the George Street cross-roads, again showing the George Hotel. After this had been demolished there was still a restaurant and bar in the building which replaced it. Known as The George Restaurant, it was a favourite haunt of undergraduates.

Alfred Street, off St. Giles, is now called Pusey Street. The shop on its north corner is unchanged but south of it houses have been demolished to make way for Pusey House—a theological college.

Looking at the entrance to Speedwell Street from the north along St. Aldate's. The buildings south of R. J. Grubb's shop were demolished to make way for the pre-war Morris Garages, which moved from the original site in Longwall Street. The St. Aldate's building, opened in 1932, cost over £80,000; the M.G. sports car took its name from the initials of the Morris Garages organisation. St. Aldate's Dairy was in business until only recently, when the land was needed for a road improvement scheme.

Park End Street in the 1880's. This photograph was taken even before the tramlines were laid. The buildings to the south of the street are as they were, but King's Motors is where the bill-boards stood then. Note the side of the Railway Hotel in the 1880 photograph: it stood exactly where The Royal Oxford Hotel stands today.

The front page from the First Oxford Times

The Oxford Times

Sixpence No. 5,752   CITY EDITION   Friday, September 5, 1969

W MOVE TO ND SOCCER OWDYISM

ning to parents

to stamp out hooliganism, the police are urging parents sters cause trouble during and after Oxford United's hes at the Manor Ground.

ford are have themselves properly, or : to the ade, Wat-

rried about a mob of ght, throw scene songs en gang up ainst visit- and march ooking for

ference on ed by Chief head of the vision, Supt. Cowley chael Brick- r Turner, anager, and y, its secre- vealed their ent miscon-

ts to ": to behave to join a come straight me. what might

: "As his ome along to and keep an

better"

d of Things quiet here many other country, but ter. We want before it gets

ent 95 per xford crowd, e supporters to see a good We are con- e these re- sters aged be- 8 who go to looking for

oxon warned uld continue nst offenders "crowd fans people in the but b' hrods

da too many behaviour, for las this season this section of een much the r. There is m local youths.

of parental he parents en- children to

the London Road stand—fans on the other three sides of the ground are always well-behaved.

Boots order

The police are now ordering fans to remove hobnail and ammunition boots and those with steel toe caps before letting them into the ground.

They also want parents to help put a stop to fans causing damage and singing obscene songs.

"These songs can be heard all round the ground and even in the London Road stand and they are disgusting," said Supt. East. "They are picked up by children as young as seven or eight who join in without realising what the words mean."

Mr. Turner said the club was worried that the songs would cause embarrassment and drive away genuine supporters.

Wanton damage at the Manor is also becoming a headache. Fans have kicked out sections of the London Road stand — last season one piece fell 20ft. and struck a woman, causing serious head injuries.

Last season the club had to repaint the lavatories at least eight times to cover up obscene words on the walls and doors. This season—only after four weeks—the painters have been called in twice.

"Looking for trouble"

Another problem is that often after matches young fans link up and march down Headington Hill in gangs towards the city centre. At one recent match about 300 formed a human crocodile and it took police nearly two hours to disperse them.

Supt. East said: "The game was quiet but it was obvious that some Oxford fans had evolved a plan to get at the visiting supporters. A good percentage of these lads were from Headington, Blackbird Leys and Cowley, and there was no need for them to go home this way. They were clearly looking for trouble."

Police believe that reserve supporters could do much to prevent trouble. Supt. East said: "If a fan says he objects to someone's language and can point him out to us, we have a chance."

One side only

Mr. Mr. Turner pointed out: "The problem is that many people turn a blind eye to this sort of thing and don't want to get involved."

A strange phenomenon is that all the trouble occurs in

Great day for the Trents

The Lord Mayor and Lady Mayoress of Oxford yesterday visited the home in Free Mile Drive of Mr. and Mrs. Albert Trent.

A telegram from the Queen arrived and Mr. Trent gave his wife Louisa a vast bouquet of flowers. These were just the high points in the couple's celebration yesterday of their diamond wedding: it was exactly 60 years since their marriage in Islington. They now have a family of two sons, five grandchildren and two great-grandchildren.

And though Mr. Trent used to be a keen bowler in Oxford with the City and County Bowls Club, Mrs. Trent put the record straight about the couple's loyalties: "We're good old Cockneys, really."

Mr. Trent is a retired dentist and he and his wife have lived in the couple's last terdau of their diamond wedding and seem to want their revenge.

Mr. Turner said the club was fully behind the police in their efforts to stop trouble. "The problem has not yet reached the heights but we just want to stop it snowballing. This club has a good reputation and we want to keep it."

Chief Supt. Coxon added: "We are always prepared for trouble and we will handle it when it occurs. But our object at present is to prevent it."

7 reported after Bury game

Seven young soccer fans were reported on Wednesday night for using obscene language during Oxford's game against Bury.

Another person was charged with an offence under the Public Order Act 1936.

A spokesman at Cowley police station said: "In future there will be a number of police officers in the crowd to deal with this type of offender."

Police are concentrating mainly on supporters who congregate in the stand behind the London Road goal.

Austin Morris plans for 'magic million' by 1973

The Austin Morris division of British Leyland Motor Corporation expects to produce 1m. vehicles a year by 1973 or 1974, Mr. George Turnbull, the managing director, said yesterday.

The division will have the capacity to produce "well over a 1m. vehicles" by the early 70's. It now employs 60,000 people in 13 different factories —including five of the six car factories in the Oxford area.

Mr. Turnbull, speaking in Birmingham, said he was confident that the new plan which had been formulated by the division would result in the magical figure being reached by 1973 or 1974 if market conditions allow it.

He said that the recruitment of university graduates would help to ensure the realisation of the plan.

200 graduates

"In future," said Mr. Turnbull," we want to be producing over 1m. vehicles, but we must have the right people to control the expansion and the

programme of the division if we are to do so."

The division was looking critically at its recruitment programme as it was determined to attract the right sort of people "from the very start."

British Leyland was engaging nearly 200 graduates this year and 135 would join the Austin Morris division.

Members of the senior and middle management had been on special courses to get some basic advice on how to interview graduates.

"There is considerable competition for the best people from the universities and we must project an attractive image to them."

"We want positive, enthusiastic and aggressive young men come and of strengthening our position as the leader of the British motor industry," said Mr. Turnbull.

The Austin Morris division is to spend £70m. to increase its production capacity by more than 120,000 units a year to more than 1m.

The creation of the Cowley

complex — the integration of Pressed Steel Fisher's car body plant and the Morris Motors car assembly plant—at a cost of around £45m. is a major part of the division's expansion programme.

This will enable the car output of Morris Motors and the M.G. works at Abingdon to total 10,000 a week.

'Great credit'

Mr. Turnbull also announced that the division had increased its production, exports and share of the home market during the six months up to the end of July.

Production was up by 15.5 per cent when compared with the corresponding period the previous year. Vehicle production went up from 538,302 to 621,480.

Exports rose by 24.5 per cent, crossing numerically up from 235,148 to 2 the division's share of the United Kingdom car market had risen from 29.2 to 30.1 per cent. "This may not sound very dramatic," said Mr. Turnbull," but the 1 per cent increase has been achieved while the market dropped by 13.9 per cent."

Commenting on the figures, he said: "They reflect great credit on the new management team at Austin Morris and on the efforts of staff and workers on the shop floor."

ST. GILES FAIR PLANS

St. Giles' Fair on Monday and Tuesday will follow its traditional pattern.

The lay-out will be as usual, with the larger machines sited between the Beaumont Street junction and the Lamb and Flag public house. Studd's, Nichols and Noyce's Gallop and Horses.

St. Giles will be closed from 1 a.m. on Sunday and the bigger attractions will move in by 8.30 a.m. from the Quarry, where the showmen have been gathering during the past week.

As usual, the Markets and Fairs Committee has allocated space near the St. John's fire court for charity stalls.

There will be diversions of several bus routes on Sunday, Monday and Tuesday.

Senior Aircraftsman gets married at Bisingshurst church

Senior Aircraftsman John eldest

Mr. Peter Crossley and Miss Susan Gillies, both of Ontario, who were married at St. Peter's Church, Wolvercote, on Wednesday

The wedding that just happened

Pay rise for 104 works police

The 104 works policemen at the three Morris factories at Cowley, who went on strike in July over their pay claim, are to get increases ranging from £2 7s. 6d. to £3 12s. 6d.

The increases, which date from July 28, have been negotiated by their union, the Transport and General Workers'. Mr. C. Clifford Small, the union's organiser in the Oxford area, who led the union's negotiators, said that the new pay structure was based on increments which varied according to service.

The maximum rate will now be payable after four years' service.

The works policemen went on strike after turning down an offer of a £2 7s. 6d. a week increase which was given to other staff employees.

The policemen sought a bigger increase because of the longer hours they work — four 12-hour shifts a week.

Forty-four will get another £3 12s. 6d.; 32 will get £2 17s. 6d. and 28 £2 7s. 6d.

With the weekly first aid allowance, the top rate for a 48-hour week is £26 5s., slightly more than the pay of the works policemen at Pressed Steel Fisher, Cowley.

And with overtime, those at the Morris factory can boost their earnings even higher.

PRIEST'S DEATH IN SEA SWIM

A former priest-in-charge of St. Alban's Church, Charles Street, Oxford, the Rev. Harry Nesbitt, has died while swimming in the sea off Malta, where he was on holiday.

Mr. Nesbitt, who was in his early fifties, had been Rector of Huntingdon for five years.

He was at St. Alban's Church for eight years, from 1946 to 1952 and previously worked with the Rev. Leslie Arnold, Vicar of St. Mary and John Church, Oxford, in Manchester.

Mr. Arnold said yesterday: "He was an ardent Scouter, and as correspondent manager of SS. Mary and John's schools he carried through on behalf of the managers, considerable reconstruction work following the 1944 Education Act."

SMALL CHILD INJURED

[h]er of a household child, Jacqueline Todd, of 22 Stott worth Path, Oxford, was taken to the Radcliffe Infirmary with head injuries on Friday week after she was in collision with a milk float.

A spokesman at the hospital said yesterday that her condition was satisfactory.

FUNERAL OF MRS. ROSA DAVIS

The funeral took place at St. Andrew's Church on Wednesday of Mrs. Rosa Jennie Davis, of 16 Lathbury Road, the widow of Prof. H. W. C. Davis who was Regius Professor of Modern History at the University from 1925 to 1928. Prof Davis was a former fellow of All Souls and Balliol.

The Rev. S. D. Faces officiated, assisted by the Rev. Godfrey Monday at the family present were Mr. and Mrs. W P C Davis, Mr. and Mrs. R C Davis and Mr. and Mrs. R H C Davis (sons) Davis and Mr. J J J Davis (grandsons); Mrs. S D. Faces (niece) and Mr. Bramley Davis (nephew).

Among others present were: the President, St. John's and Mrs. Southern, Prof and Mrs V H. Galbraith, Dr. R. W. Hunt (representing Balliol College), Dr. D. R. Harden, Prof M. C. Fowther, Mr. C. las, Mr. and Mrs. D. Pilkington, the Rev J. R. Reynolds, Mrs.

The front page from one of the latest Oxford Times

Only one corner of The High Street end of Longwall has changed. A barber-cum-umbrella-mender has disappeared and now a larger yellow stone building stands in its place. Note that two three-storey houses on the west side of Longwall have not changed at all since the end of the last century.

The same tree in St. Mary Magdalen's churchyard still shades the Magdalen and Broad Street corner. William Baker's old premises can be seen clearly on the other side of the street—shades drawn to protect the window displays from the bright afternoon sun.

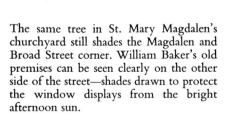

38

Until very recently, the whole west side of Longwall Street was taken up with little houses, as shown in this early photograph. Most of these houses still exist, somewhat shuttered up but still imparting an atmosphere of calm and agelessness. Some have been replaced by the Sacher building of New College.

Oliver the Printer was still in George Street at the end of the last century when this photograph was taken and his shop is clearly seen. Now, however, he has had to move to the south side of the street to make way for the wartime Municipal Restaurant.

Little Clarendon Street at the turn of the century looked like the top photograph— an ordinary little street of houses and a few shops. To the left were the big houses of Wellington Square. Now, however, it is the 'in' street of Oxford with shops selling, amongst other things, kitchen gadgets which would not be out of place in an Edwardian household. The big new building is a block of rooms for post-graduates of Somerville College.

To the east of Worcester Street, behind a high wall, lay the terminal wharf of the Oxford Canal. It was overlooked by the old Oxfordshire County Constabulary and the County Council offices. The warehouse there was built actually over the canal, so that goods could be unloaded from the narrow boats, whatever the weather. Until its demolition to make way for Nuffield College (see right) the wharf yard was used as a car park, access being gained to it by a gateway in the tall, crumbling wall—made of local sandstone—which extended most of the way along New Road to Queen Street.

A pre-twentieth century picture of George Street, showing Lisemore's, the store of a dealer in earthenware and domestic china. For many years he sold his goods at St. Giles' Fair, setting them out in a display on the ground on a site opposite the corner of Pusey Street. His shop and warehouse were pulled down to erect a cinema—The Oxford Cinematograph Theatre—which was said to be 'one of the best equipped and most comfortable in the Kingdom'. There were continuous performances from 2.30 p.m. and the programme changed on Mondays and Thursdays. From 6 p.m. there was an orchestra; admission was 1s. 0d. or 3s. 6d. This was demolished in 1935 to make way for a new entry to Gloucester Street. The present ABC Cinema, until recently The Ritz, was built shortly afterwards.

King Edward Street did not exist when the above photograph was taken—there was, instead, a row of shops which have now all disappeared. Now 106 High Street is the entrance to the Tackley Hotel and Williams Deacon's Bank occupied what was Goundrey's—later Launchbury's the confectioners and tobacconists. The next building has been pulled down to make way for the far less attractive architecture which houses the Abbey National Building Society, but Savory and Moore occupies the surviving east corner building of King Edward Street.

The above photograph shows to what extent The Plain has changed. Taken prior to the building of the tramway, it shows the full extent of the toll-gates and the toll-gate keeper's cottage. Behind this is an old graveyard, now disappeared, giving way to a pleasant central area of flowers and trees and a very busy road junction. Now Robert Maxwell's bookshop has replaced the row of shops to the left of the picture, whilst the Victoria fountain was built at the end of the last century on the site of the toll-gate keeper's cottage.

Most of the west side of Cornmarket from St. Michael's Street to Carfax has changed in the last fifty years and some of it has changed twice. In a previous photograph, the Clarendon Hotel has been clearly distinguished and here it is possible to see what a great difference the loss of Carfax church and Falkners has made. When the latter was demolished a great Gothic shop was erected. This became the famous grocery shop of Grimbly Hughes, later taken over by Jackson's of Piccadilly. Trade, however, had been affected so much by supermarkets that it was decided to close down completely and Littlewood's built a modern store on the site. Also comparatively new are Burton's shop, the Co-operative carpet showrooms (until very recently the 'Carfax Assembly Rooms') and the Midland Bank.

Park End Street in the 1920's was a very busy thoroughfare, much narrower than today. Its shops included a barber with a genuine 'candy-stick' pole. Also evident was a boarding house and a garage for forty cars. Now the boarding house and barber have gone, leaving a modern block of flats and offices with new shops and two garages underneath them. Gone, too, are the picturesque gas lamps and in their place now stand the gallows of the modern sodium lamps.

A view north along Worcester Street, showing the establishment of W. & T. Avery who have been making and repairing scales since 1730. They were also licensed to repair and service the municipal weigh-bridges.

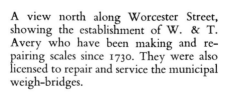

B. H. Blackwell started bookselling in St. Clements in the 1840's. The present bookshop, in Broad Street, was opened in 1879, by the grandfather of Sir Basil Blackwell, who is now president of the largest bookselling firm in the world. The top photograph shows the shop with its beautifully preserved architecture and neighbouring buildings. Still in Broad Street, basically the same today, Blackwell's have extended to occupy number 48 to 51 plus the building above the renovated public house, The White Horse. Behind its modest façade, and even beneath the gardens of adjacent Trinity College, the shop is the centre of a vast organisation. Beyond Blackwell's, the old buildings have been demolished to make way for the New Bodleian Library and book stack, one of the five Copyright Libraries of the United Kingdom.

St. Aldate's, looking south. Only Christ
Church, two buildings above, and the
buildings below the Post Office are recog-
nisable; the rest—little shops, offices and
homes and the tram lines—have all been
swept away to make room for modern
buildings and smoother roads. No clock
was above the doorway to the Post Office
then . . . time didn't matter so much, it
seems. No photograph illustrates in such
an undramatic way how much Oxford has
changed over the last 100 years. Has it, one
wonders, changed for the better?

I *Evan Evans, D.D.*

Vice-Chancellor of the University of Oxford, in pursuance of Privileges confirmed to the said University by divers Acts of Parliament, Do hereby permit and authorize, give full License, Power, and Authority unto *Dr Anson, Jane, Randolph Hotel St Mary Magdalen* for *herself* only to sell, by retail or otherwise, any Sort of good and wholesome Wine or Wines allowed by law to be sold, for the Space of one Year from the *21st* Day of December, 1887.

Given under my hand this *20th* Day of *December* in the 4*5th* Year of the Reign of our Sovereign Lady Victoria, by the Grace of God Queen of the United Kingdom of Great Britain and Ireland, Defender of the Faith, and so forth; and in the Year of our Lord 1887.

E. Evans, Vice-Chancellor

N.B.—Every Person selling Wine without License within the said University, and Precincts thereof, forefeits, for every Offence, the Sum of *Five Pounds.* 17 Geo. II. c. 40.

Old advertisements are a fascinating source of historical records—especially those of products common during the last 100 years. On this page are shown three advertisements, interesting if only for their style—amateur beside today's sophisticated 'ads'.

The bottom left photograph is of the first licence granted to the Randolph Hotel allowing it to sell alcohol. In common with all such licences of this time, it was issued by the University, rather than by the City authorities.

In September 1912, French aviator Garros set up a new altitude record of 16,400 feet over France and a month later Oxford's first air display was scheduled to take place on Port Meadow. Arranged by the Grahame-White Aviation Company, the display had to be cancelled at the last moment because, although permission had been given to use the Meadow by the Civic and University authorities, it was found that—by ancient statute—no part of the Meadow could be cordoned off for any reason, it being all 'Common Land'. The Oxford Times used this as an excuse for a scathing attack on the few 'very prosperous people' who were the only people to benefit from the land as it then stood. Apart from a fatal air crash in 1912, little aviation news was made in Oxford until the Oxford City Council bought some land at Kidlington to develop as a civil airport. It was used almost solely by the Oxford Aeroplane Club, who moved there from the old Witney Aerodrome, until the outbreak of war in 1939 when, in common with all civil airfields, it was taken over by the Crown.

The R.A.F. first used it as a flying school; but from 1942 until April 1943, when it reverted back to a training station for pilots of powered aeroplanes, it was used as a glider pilot training school. In October 1944 it again saw gliders as pilots were trained there for the Normandy landings and the crossing of the Rhine. After the war the airfield was used again by the Oxford Aeroplane Club and has now grown into the world-famous Oxford Air Training School. Nowadays the sight of aircraft over Oxford is no novelty. Many times a day the buzz of light aircraft from Kidlington, the screech of R.A.F. VC 10's and Belfasts, and the roar of Hercules and Argosys makes Oxford's air traffic far noisier than the quiet days before the First World War.

By permission of
The Vice-Chancellor,
The Mayor, The Sheriff, and
The Freemen of Oxford.

To be held at the

PORT MEADOW

FLYING GROUND
OXFORD
(Weather Permitting)
Entrances at Walton Road Bridge and Black Bridge.

FLYING EXHIBITIONS
SPEED TESTS and
ALTITUDE FLIGHTS
by Well-known Aviators,
Including
Mrs. STOCKS
Mr. M. DESOUTTER
Mr. LOUIS NOEL
Mr. J. L. TRAVERS
Mr. RICHARD T. GATES
and
Mr. C. GRAHAME-WHITE

Passenger Flights from £3 - 3 - 0
may be booked in advance. Early application should be made as the number of Passenger Flights is limited.

Tickets should be purchased in advance from the Agents,
JAS. RUSSELL & Co. 120. High St., Oxford

Further Particulars from the Organisers
The Grahame-White Aviation Co. Ltd.
The London Aerodrome. Hendon. London. N.W.

FLYING AT OXFORD

FIRST OXFORD
AVIATION MEETING
THURSDAY, OCT. 24th, 1912

At 2.30 p.m.   ADMISSION 1s. and 2s. 6d. (Paddock);   MOTORS (Paddock Enclosure) 2s. 6d. (Includes Chauffeur)
Motor Entrance at Walton Road Bridge only.

The regular Oxford Fire Brigade came into being after the wartime National Fire Service was disbanded in 1948. Before the Second World War, the Oxford Volunteer Fire Brigade dealt with fires in Oxford. The above photograph—taken at the turn of the century in Broad Street—shows the colourful dress and simple equipment of this force.

Now, the regular fire brigade employs about 85 full-time men as well as 18 'retained' men who can be called in when emergencies require their services. The brigade has eight appliances costing an average of £8,000—a far cry from the Edwardian equipment. The modern photograph shows the new Slade Park station with three recent tenders.

The River Thames, or Isis as it is called at Oxford, was probably the direct reason for Oxford's situation. Even the name suggests the reason, for, with the river much wider, shallower and more difficult to bridge than it is today, fords were of the utmost military and commercial importance. The original ford—by which oxen were driven across—is believed to have been at Ferry Hinksey. However, there is some evidence that it was situated at Osney. Wherever it was, the Anglo-Saxon Chronicle tells us that Edward the Elder, son of King Alfred the Great, took possession of the land on which the present city stands and fortified it to guard the ford across the boundary between the Danelaw and his own kingdom of Wessex. Even in living memory, the Thames was liable to severe flooding. Owing to its sluggish current, a hard winter would turn the river into a playground. In 1891 a sheep was roasted on the ice above Iffley and a coach-and-four was driven down it.

The photograph at the top of the page shows the station approach during the great flood of 1894, when havoc was caused by heavy rainfall, on the nights of November 11 and 12.

At the bottom of the page is a photograph of the Isis at the turn of the century when it was only fifty years since the river had been a vital link with London (although not always navigable for the whole length).

Now, modern roads and railways have made it commercially obsolete; but every year undergraduates show their rowing prowess upon it while visitors and townspeople alike discover the relaxing pursuits of punting and canoeing along its wide stream

THE EXCURSION-PLAN OF OXFORD,

PRICE FOURPENCE.

(The places marked thus * are the points of greatest attraction to a Visitor.)

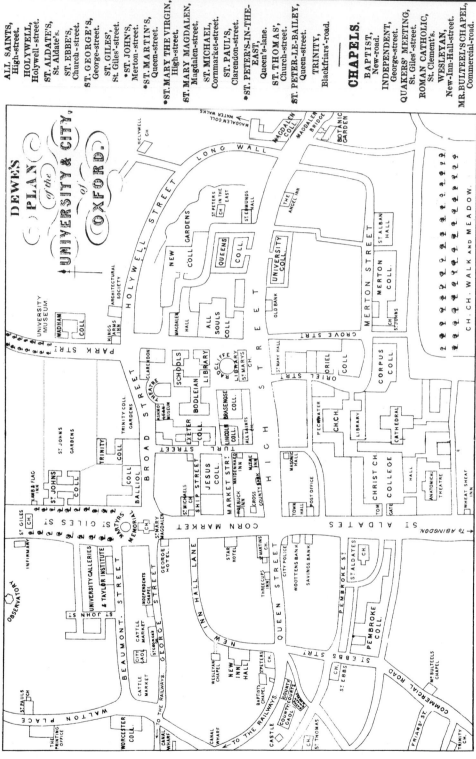

COLLEGES.

*ALL SOULS, High-street.
BALLIOL, Broad-street.
BRASENOSE, Radcliffe-square.
*CHRIST CHURCH, St. Aldate's.
CORPUS CHRISTI, Merton-street.
EXETER, Turl-street.
JESUS, Turl-street.
LINCOLN, Turl-street.
*MAGDALEN, High-street.
*MERTON, Merton-street.
*NEW COLLEGE, New College-lane.
ORIEL, Oriel-street.
PEMBROKE, St. Aldate's.
*QUEEN'S, High-street.
*ST. JOHN'S, St. Giles'-street.
*TRINITY, Broad-street.
*UNIVERSITY, High-street.
WADHAM, Park-street.
*WORCESTER, Beaumont-street.

HALLS.

EXETER, Turl-street.
MAGDALEN, New College-lane.
NEW-INN-HALL, New-Inn-Hall-street.
*ST. ALBAN, Merton-street.
ST. EDMUND, Queen's-lane.
ST. MARY, Oriel-street.

PUBLIC BUILDINGS.

*ANATOMICAL MUSEUM, Christ Church.
*ARCHITECTURAL MUSEUM, Holywell-street.
*ASHMOLEAN MUSEUM, Broad-street.
BATHS (PUBLIC WARM), New-road.
*BODLEIAN LIBRARY, Schools-quadrangle.
CLARENDON BUILDINGS, Broad-street.
COUNTY HALL AND GAOL, New-road.
*DIVINITY SCHOOL, Schools-quadrangle.
*GEOLOGICAL MUSEUM, Broad-street.

MUSEUMS, GALLERIES, INSTITUTIONS, AND OFFICES.

MARKETS.—Meat, Vegetable, and Corn,—High street.
*MARTYRS' MEMORIAL, Magdalen-street.
MILITIA DEPOT AND ARMOURY, New-road.
*MODERN LANGUAGES, INSTITUTE FOR St. Giles'-street.
*MUSEUM, NEW, UNIVERSITY, in the Public Parks,
*PICTURE AND SCULPTURE GALLERIES Beaumont-street.
POST-OFFICE, St. Aldate's.
POLICE-STATION, St. Aldate's.
PRINTING-OFFICE, UNIVERSITY, Clarendon street.

PUBLIC FREE LIBRARY, St. Aldate's.
RADCLIFFE INFIRMARY, St. Giles'-street.
*RADCLIFFE LIBRARY, Radcliffe-square.
RADCLIFFE OBSERVATORY, St. Giles'-street.
RAILWAY-STATIONS, G. W. and N. W., New-road.
SCHOOLS, PUBLIC EXAMINATION, Schools-quadrangle.
*SHELDONIAN THEATRE, Broad-street.
TOWN-HALL AND COUNCIL-CHAMBER, St. Aldate's.

CHURCHES.

*CATHEDRAL, Christ Church.
Parish Churches.
ALL SAINTS, High-street.
HOLYWELL, Holywell-street.
ST. ALDATE'S, St. Aldate's.
ST. EBBE'S, Church-street.
ST. GEORGE'S, George-street.
ST. GILES' St. Giles'-street.
*ST. JOHN'S, Merton-street.
*ST. MARTIN'S, Queen-street.
*ST. MARY THE VIRGIN, High-street.
*ST. MARY MAGDALEN, Magdalen-street.
ST. MICHAEL, Cornmarket-street.
ST. PAUL'S, Clarendon-street.
*ST. PETER'S-IN-THE-EAST, Queen's-lane.
ST. THOMAS, Church-street.
*ST. PETER-LE-BAILEY, Queen-street.
TRINITY, Blackfriars'-road.

CHAPELS.

BAPTIST, New-road.
INDEPENDENT, George-street.
QUAKERS' MEETING, St. Giles'-street.
ROMAN CATHOLIC, St. Clement's.
WESLEYAN, New-Inn-Hall-street.
MR.BULTEEL'SCHAPEL, Commercial-road.

GARDENS AND PUBLIC WALKS.

*BOTANIC GARDENS, High-street.
*CHRIST CHURCH BROAD WALK.
*CHRIST CHURCH MEADOW AND WALKS, by the river Isis.
*MAGDALEN GROVE AND WATER-WALKS.
*MERTON COLLEGE GARDENS.
*NEW COLLEGE GARDENS.
PARKS, a public walk to the North.
*ST. JOHN'S COLLEGE GARDENS.
*TRINITY COLLEGE GARDENS.
*WORCESTER COLLEGE GARDENS.

Published by John Dewe.

Oxford as it was in 1860

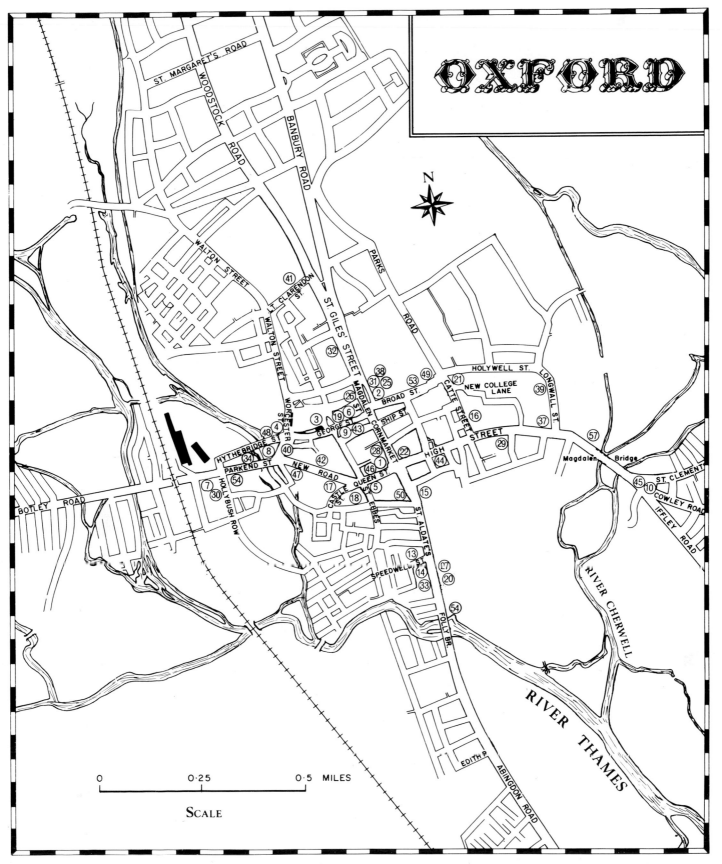

The numbers on this map refer to the pages on which illustrations of the various locations appear.

The great tower of Magdalen College at the turn of the century

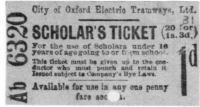

Memory Lane